MAKE AND KEEP

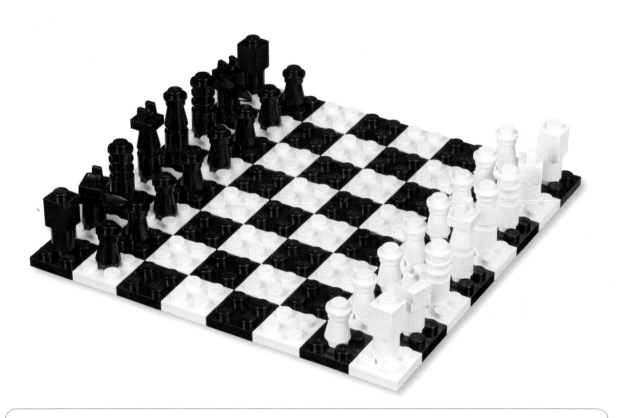

CONTENTS

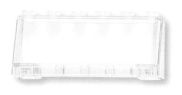

2x6x2 WINDSHIELD

1x2 BRICK

1x2x2 BRICK

2x2x3 BRICK

2x2x3 SLOPE

USEFUL PIECES

When building practical models, stability is key. Use lots of square or rectangular bricks to build a solid base before adding fancy and decorative pieces. To make your models exciting, build them up with different types of pieces, including bricks, plates, slopes, dishes, arches, and cones. Here are some useful pieces to keep in your tool kit!

1x2 SLOPE

1x2x3 SLOPE

1x2 PLATE WITH HANDLED BAR

1x2 PLATE WITH BAR

1x6 PLATE

2x8 PLATE

1x6 TILE

1x6 BRICK

1x2 BRICK

1x1 BRICK

1x1 BRICK

HINGES
Clip and bar plates are an easy way to build a hinge. Hinges are great for adding moving parts, like a lid that opens and shuts. (See Pirate Treasure Chest, pp.12–13)

2x2 CURVED BRICK

1x4 BRICK

2x2 PLATE

1x2 TILE

1x2 TEXTURED BRICK

COOL COLORS
Choose your colors carefully. Do you want your model to match something in your house or room?

2x3 BRICK

2x2 BRICK

2x2 INVERTED SLOPE

2x4 ANGLED PLATE

2x4 DOUBLE ANGLED PLATE

4x4 CURVED PLATE

2x2 FLOWER

2x2 FLOWER

1x1 ROUND BRICK

1x1 PLATE WITH VERTICAL CLIP

1x1 TOOTH PLATE

1x1 HEADLIGHT BRICK

2x2 CURVED BRICK

BAMBOO PLANT

1x1 ROUND PLATE

1x1 SLOPE

1x1 CONE

1x1 TOOTH PLATE

CLEAN CURVES
Curved pieces will help build models with rounded edges.

1x3x2 HALF ARCH

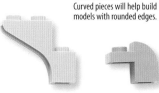

1x2 CURVED HALF ARCH

VEGETATION DECORATION
Small pieces, such as flowers, plants, or transparent plates, can decorate simple builds like a picture frame. (See Flower Power, p.15)

SMALL PLANT LEAVES

LEGO® TECHNIC T-BAR

THINK ABOUT WHAT YOU WANT TO MAKE, SELECT YOUR BRICKS, AND GET BUILDING!

1x3x2 CURVED HALF ARCH

2x2 ANGLED CORNER BRICK

2x2 ROUND BRICK

1x3 CAR DOOR

2x2 BRICK WITH WHEEL ARCH

2x2 ROUND PLATE

2x2 RADAR DISH

WIDE RIM, WIDE TIRE, AND 2x2 AXLE PLATE WITH 1 PIN

2x2 ROUND BRICK

2x2 DOMED BRICK

LEGO TECHNIC CROSS AXLE 4

1x2 HINGED BRICK AND 2x2 HINGED PLATE

SPECIAL PIECES
If you have an unusual piece in your collection, invent a model to include it in! This white girder (below) works well in a space-age display stand. (See Space Station Display, p.9)

CONNECTING PIECES
Pieces that have holes and extra studs are a great way to connect different sections of your model together—and provide places to attach decorative pieces.

4x4 ROUND PLATE

1x6 CURVED BAR WITH STUDS

4x4x2 CONE

1x6x5 GIRDER

DESK ORGANIZERS

Sort out your stationery with a LEGO® desk organizer! Before you start, think about what you want to keep in your desk organizer: Pens, rulers, erasers? Do you need drawers? How big should it be? A desk organizer should be practical and sturdy, but it can also brighten up a workspace, so add decoration in your favorite theme or color scheme!

CASTLE DESK ORGANIZER

This cool desk organizer has boxes for your pens and pencils, a drawer for smaller stationery—and it looks like a miniature castle! Start with the drawer and make sure it is big enough to fit whatever you want to store inside.

STEP-BY-STEP

After you've built the drawer, make a box that fits neatly around it. Once the box is high enough to cover the drawer, top it off with some plates, adding decoration and open boxes.

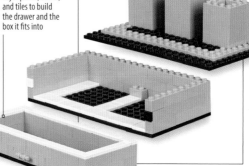

Layer plates, bricks, and tiles to build the drawer and the box it fits into

Need even more room for your stationery collection? Build boxes in various widths and heights

Simple, square open-topped boxes hold pencils and pens

Decorate your desk organizer with plates in contrasting colors

FRONT VIEW

Gray, white, and black bricks are good for a castle theme, but you can use any colors you want!

You could use a large plate to build the base of the drawer, but several small plates work if you reinforce them

Build a plate with handled bar into the drawer front so you can open it

SEA MONSTER

Scare away stationery stealers with a sea monster desk organizer! Begin with a basic box shape, build in dividers, then add the features that make a monster of the deep. Can you think of other creatures that could keep your stationery safe? Have a go at making those, too!

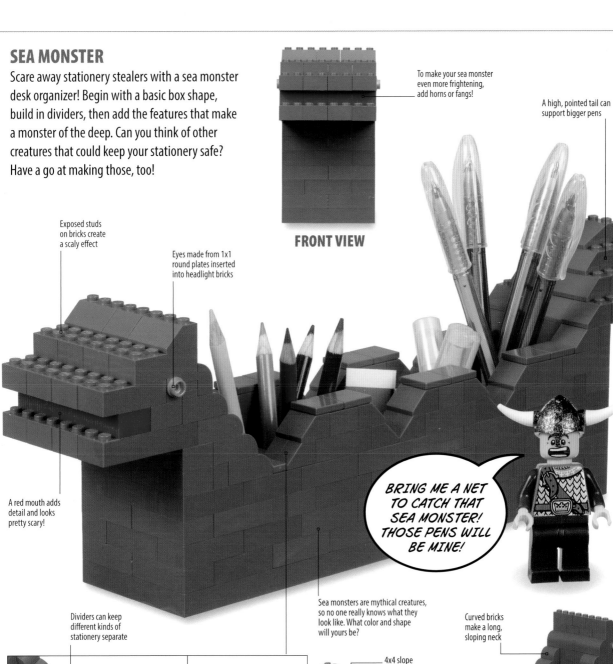

To make your sea monster even more frightening, add horns or fangs!

FRONT VIEW

A high, pointed tail can support bigger pens

Exposed studs on bricks create a scaly effect

Eyes made from 1x1 round plates inserted into headlight bricks

A red mouth adds detail and looks pretty scary!

BRING ME A NET TO CATCH THAT SEA MONSTER! THOSE PENS WILL BE MINE!

Dividers can keep different kinds of stationery separate

Sea monsters are mythical creatures, so no one really knows what they look like. What color and shape will yours be?

Curved bricks make a long, sloping neck

4x4 slope

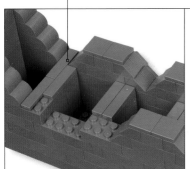

SEA SLOPES

The sea monster's humped body and pointed tail get their smooth shape from slopes topped with tiles. You could also create humps by stacking bricks in stepped layers.

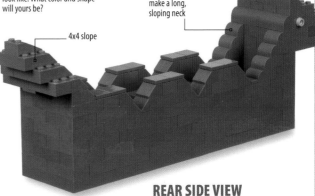

REAR SIDE VIEW

TRUCK ORGANIZER

Your desk organizer can look like anything you like. Why not take inspiration from everyday objects as with this colorful truck? It can deliver a truckload of stationery straight to your desk! What are your favorite things? What kind of shapes would make a good desk organizer? Try building one based on a car, an animal, or a spaceship. Go ahead—it's your workspace!

Add lots of contrasting colors to brighten up your workspace!

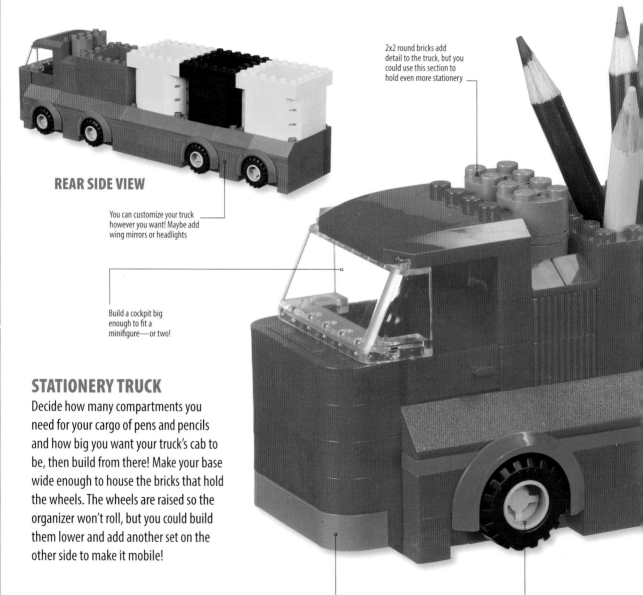

2x2 round bricks add detail to the truck, but you could use this section to hold even more stationery

REAR SIDE VIEW

You can customize your truck however you want! Maybe add wing mirrors or headlights

Build a cockpit big enough to fit a minifigure—or two!

STATIONERY TRUCK

Decide how many compartments you need for your cargo of pens and pencils and how big you want your truck's cab to be, then build from there! Make your base wide enough to house the bricks that hold the wheels. The wheels are raised so the organizer won't roll, but you could build them lower and add another set on the other side to make it mobile!

Curved pieces give the front of the truck a smooth shape. Or you could use slopes or angled plates

2x2 wheels fit into 2x2 bricks with wheel arches

SIDE VIEW

A brick separator could come in handy when you're building your organizer!

Compartments can be varying sizes, depending on what you want to store in them

*HANG ON...
IF I'M IN HERE,
WHO'S DRIVING
THIS THING?!*

Large buckets look like a real truck's cargo!

Try using curved bricks instead of angular bricks to give your compartments a different look

This side sticks out from the cab so it can accommodate the wheels

TOP VIEW

MINIFIGURE DISPLAY

Be proud of your minifigures! Show off your building skills by making a display stand to house your growing collection. You can add to your stand every time you get a new minifigure. You can even build stands in different styles to display minifigures from different LEGO themes!

BUILDING BRIEF
Objective: Build display stands
Use: Storage, decoration
Features: Sturdy enough to hold minifigures
Extras: Doors, moving parts

DISPLAY STAND

You can make a display stand with simple bricks and plates. Build a basic structure that is stable and balanced. Then use special or interesting bricks to add detail. Choose exciting colors, or maybe use a color that matches your bedroom. It's up to you!

REAR VIEW

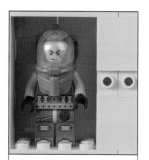

NEW HEIGHTS
A height of five bricks is tall enough to fit most minifigures nicely, but if yours has a large hat or helmet you may need to make the level higher.

A mix of minifigures makes your display stand interesting to look at

Use pieces like curved half arches if you have them

You will know straight away if one of your figures is missing!

Unusual shapes built with half arches. Inverted slopes would work, too

Use plates, not tiles, so your figures can't fall off

Headlight bricks could hold tiles that correspond to minifigures

NOW'S MY CHANCE TO MAKE A RUN FOR IT!

Accessorize to match the theme of your stand. Add antennas, or some droids!

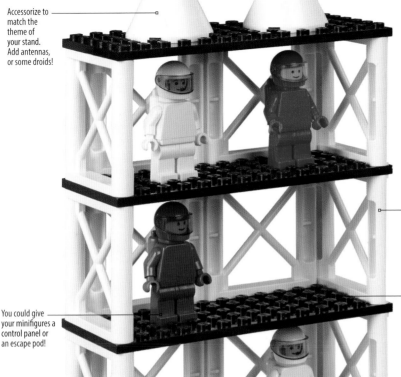

SPACE STATION DISPLAY

This space station stand is out of this world! White girders make this display stand look like something from outer space. If you decide to use fun and unusual bricks for your walls, make sure they're tall enough to house your minifigures!

Build the stand as wide as you need to contain all your minifigures

If you don't have a big enough plate, overlap smaller plates to whatever size you want

5...4...3...2...1... BLAST OFF! WHOA, WAIT FOR ME!

You could give your minifigures a control panel or an escape pod!

Girders come in a few LEGO® Town sets. Use any specialized bricks you have that fit your theme

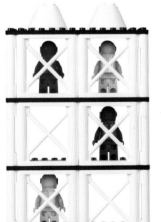

REAR VIEW

WORK IT OUT

How many minifigures do you want to display in your stand? Once you know, build each layer accordingly using pieces that fit your theme. These white girders look really space-age.

Choose colors to match your theme. For an underwater theme, use blue and green. What else can you think of?

If you don't have these pieces, try building with transparent bricks like windows—they look great as part of a space theme!

BOXES

Are your LEGO pieces all over the place? Pencils scattered over your desk? These boxes are the answer. Think about what you will put in your box and how big it should be. It will need to be strong and stable to hold all your treasures. Choose a simple color scheme and design—or just go crazy with your imagination. Don't feel boxed in!

FRONT SIDE VIEW

SHINY BOX

This box will brighten up any desk—and make it tidy, too! The bottom is made of large plates, and the sides are built up with interlocking bricks and topped with tiles for a smooth finish. The lid is built as a wall that is slightly larger than the top of the box.

A row of shiny tiles finishes off the box lid

Choose your favorite colors for your box

You could increase the height of your box so you have more room inside

NOT SURE THESE COLORS ARE THE BEST FOR A GOOD NIGHT'S SLEEP!

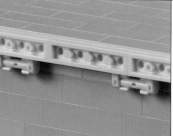

JOINTS THAT JOIN

The hinges are made from pairs of plates with bars and plates with horizontal clips. They are held in place by a row of tiles on top. To increase stability so you can use the box for longer, add more hinges.

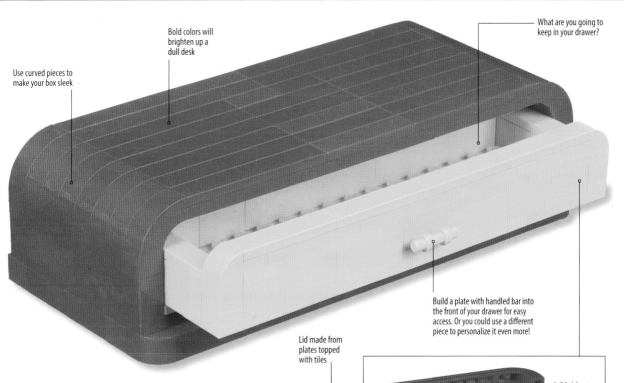

Use curved pieces to
make your box sleek

Bold colors will
brighten up a
dull desk

What are you going to
keep in your drawer?

Build a plate with handled bar into
the front of your drawer for easy
access. Or you could use a different
piece to personalize it even more!

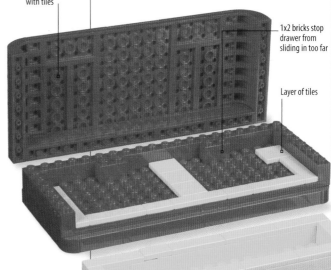

Lid made from
plates topped
with tiles

1x2 bricks stop
drawer from
sliding in too far

Layer of tiles

COOL CURVES

Boxes don't need to be boxy—they
can be curvy, too! Use curved pieces to
create your desired shape. Make the
drawer first, then build the box around
it. Finally, create a base as a wall
turned on its side. Use bricks with side
studs to attach the base to the box.

Curved half arch

FRONT VIEW

SLIDING DRAWERS

To help the drawer slide easily, fix some tiles to the base
of the box. These will create a smooth layer so the
drawer won't catch on the studs as it slides in and out.

TREASURE CHEST

You can make boxes in all shapes and sizes—and to match any theme you like! Maybe you want a medieval wooden trunk with big metal locks to store your knight minifigures. Or a hi-tech, zero-gravity space capsule for your astronauts and aliens. Use different colors to style your box, and remember, the lid doesn't have to be flat!

BUILDING BRIEF
Objective: Create fantasy boxes
Use: Storage, play
Features: Hinged lid, drawers
Extras: Secret compartments, decorations

PIRATE TREASURE CHEST

This treasure chest has a secret drawer at the bottom for hiding your most precious LEGO pieces (or any other treasures)! First, the lower half is built around the sliding drawer. Then the top half is constructed on top of that, with a hinged lid, built sideways. The more hinges you use, the more stable the lid will be!

A layer of plates divides the secret drawer from the chest above it

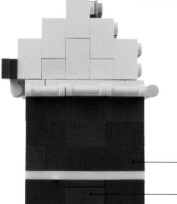

Overlap bricks for stability

Press on this secret brick and the drawer will slide out the other side!

Use different colors to theme your box—brown and yellow look like a pirate's treasure chest

SIDE VIEW

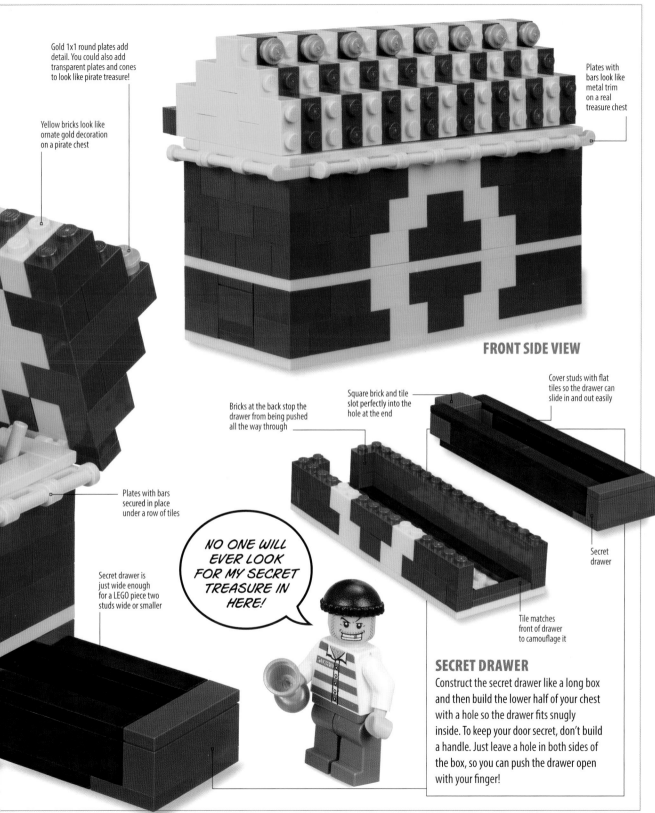

Gold 1x1 round plates add detail. You could also add transparent plates and cones to look like pirate treasure!

Yellow bricks look like ornate gold decoration on a pirate chest

Plates with bars look like metal trim on a real treasure chest

FRONT SIDE VIEW

Plates with bars secured in place under a row of tiles

Bricks at the back stop the drawer from being pushed all the way through

Square brick and tile slot perfectly into the hole at the end

Cover studs with flat tiles so the drawer can slide in and out easily

Secret drawer

NO ONE WILL EVER LOOK FOR MY SECRET TREASURE IN HERE!

Secret drawer is just wide enough for a LEGO piece two studs wide or smaller

Tile matches front of drawer to camouflage it

SECRET DRAWER

Construct the secret drawer like a long box and then build the lower half of your chest with a hole so the drawer fits snugly inside. To keep your door secret, don't build a handle. Just leave a hole in both sides of the box, so you can push the drawer open with your finger!

PICTURE FRAMES

Say cheese! How about building something to display your special pictures? You can use photos of your favorite LEGO models or treasured pictures of family and friends. Once you have a basic frame you can decorate it any way you want. You can even change the theme of your frame whenever you change the photo!

BUILDING BRIEF
Objective: Make frames for pictures
Use: Display your favorite pictures
Features: Sturdy frame, ability to stand
Extras: Multi-frames, themed frames, different shaped frames

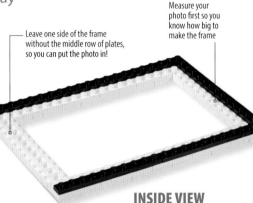

Measure your photo first so you know how big to make the frame

Leave one side of the frame without the middle row of plates, so you can put the photo in!

INSIDE VIEW

BASIC FRAME

If you want your photo to be the main attraction, keep the frame simple. Use interlocking rows of plates to make two identical rectangles. A middle layer of one-stud-wide plates holds the two rectangles together and creates a gap to slide the photo in.

Add an angle plate to the top of the stand to make it more stable against the frame

REAR SIDE VIEW

Use a plate and a clip and bar hinge to build a stand

You could alternate the colors of the plates for a cool effect

SIDE VIEWS

I SURE MISS THE GANG FROM THE OLD NEIGHBORHOOD!

FLOWER POWER

Now that you have the basic frame, you can get creative! Do you like flowers? Make them into a pattern to frame your pretty picture. You could also add some foliage or even a microbutterfly. Putting pieces at different angles creates an interesting pattern and helps fit more pieces on.

Use pieces that match your chosen theme

Use pretty flowers in your favorite colors

These radar dishes and transparent plates look really space-age

SPACE AGE

Why not decorate your frame to match your picture? This space frame has lots of translucent pieces and even a spaceman minifigure! To make the frame fit a portrait photo, simply move the position of the stands at the back of the frame.

Clip minifigures to bricks with side studs to add them to your frame!

Make extra pieces stick out to change the frame shape

Think of other pieces that would add to the jungle theme. Maybe a rope bridge or a mini waterfall?

JUNGLE FEVER

Add different colored bricks to your frame to match your theme. Use brown pieces for a jungle theme and add lots of green foliage. You could even add animal figures. Go wild!

MOSAICS

Mosaics are the art of making pictures or patterns from small pieces of material, such as glass, stone...or LEGO bricks! First, plan how you want your mosaic to look. Will it lie flat or stand upright? Will it let through light? Will it be 3-D? You will have your own LEGO art gallery in no time!

BASEPLATE
A 16x16 baseplate supports these flag mosaics, but you can build your mosaic on any size base you like! You could also attach several plates together if you don't have the right size.

FUN FLAGS
Get patriotic and make your country's flag into a LEGO mosaic! These Union Jack designs are made from 1x1 bricks, with a few wider bricks where larger blocks of color appear.

Use wider bricks for less detailed flags—it will save you some time!

Your flag doesn't have to be in the traditional colors—go color crazy!

1x1 and 1x2 bricks are stacked like a wall to make this simple design

1x1 bricks help put lots of detail into your mosaic

FLOWER ART
Say it with LEGO flowers! This flower mosaic stands upright to look like two flowers growing against a clear blue sky. Tall slopes form a stable base to hold the mosaic up.

WIDER BASE
Toward the bottom of the mosaic, an extra layer of bricks is built into the design to provide extra support for the base. The ledge is only visible on the back.

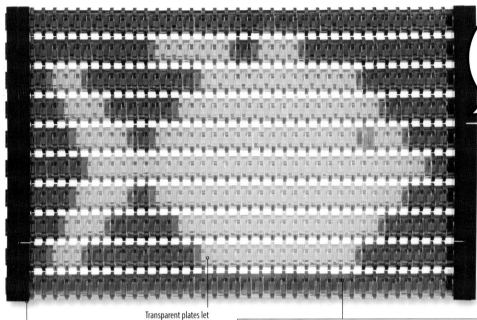

I KEEP SWIMMING, BUT I JUST CAN'T SEEM TO GET PAST THESE END PLATES!

MARINE MOSAIC

This mosaic is entirely made from transparent 1x1 round plates. Ten rows have been carefully planned and assembled to make a floating yellow fish! Long black plates frame the rows.

Transparent plates let light through, so the mosaic seems to glow!

CONSTRUCTION

The design of this mosaic takes careful planning. Transparent plates are stacked according to the pattern, then the stacks are attached on their sides to the end plates.

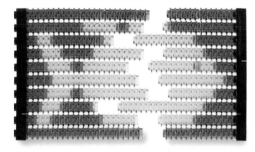

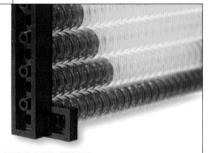

SUPPORT STAND

Add small plates at right angles to the end plate at both bottom corners. These allow the mosaic to stand up vertically, like a picture frame. If your mosaic is smaller, it will be even more stable.

ORANGE FISH

If you don't have enough transparent round plates to make an entire mosaic, it doesn't matter. You can mix and match! This orange aquatic artwork includes white round plates, too. You can include 1x1 square plates as well!

3-D MOSAICS

Mosaics don't always have to be flat. If you have bricks in different shapes and sizes, you could try adding 3-D elements to your LEGO mosaics to make them really stand out! First choose what picture you want to create, then decide which features will work best in 3-D. What do you want to draw the most attention to?

DID YOU REALLY HAVE TO DRAW EVEN MORE ATTENTION TO MY EARS?

Layer bricks at different heights to add perspective

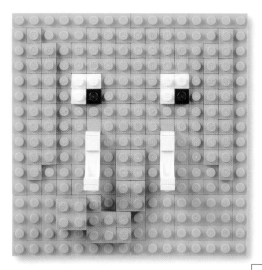

FRONT VIEW

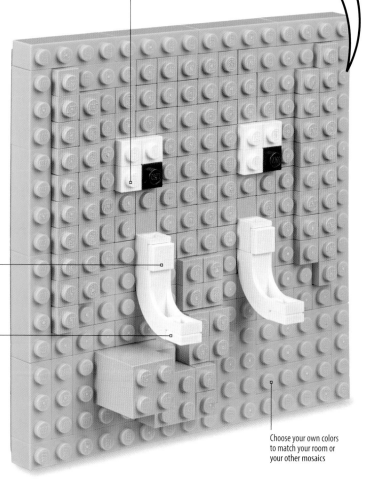

White 1x1 tile covers the exposed stud on headlight brick

Choose your own colors to match your room or your other mosaics

TUSK TASK
The elephant's protruding tusks really bring the mosaic to life! They are made from curved half arches, which attach to the green background with white headlight bricks.

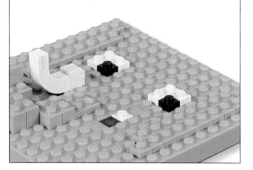

ELEPHANT
What is your favorite animal? Try making its likeness in 3-D! A 16x16 plate forms the base of this mosaic. The baseplate is completely covered in bricks, which form a green background and a basic gray elephant head shape. More bricks and plates are added to make the 3-D features.

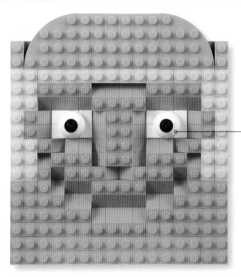

FRONT VIEW

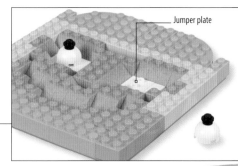

Jumper plate

EYE-POPPING

You don't have to stick to square bricks for your mosaics! Here, the eyes are made from domed bricks and black round plates. The domed bricks attach to white jumper plates.

Curved plates form the rounded sides of the girl's green hat

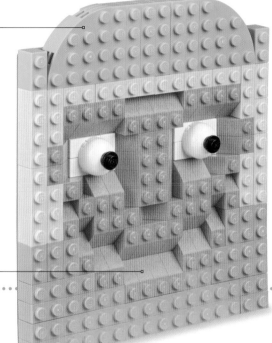

FUNNY FACE

Don't restrict yourself to square bricks! Think about how you can form 3-D details with all different kinds of pieces. This girl's facial features are almost entirely formed from pink slopes! Used this way, the pieces create a cool, crazy-looking mosaic style.

Arrange opposite-facing slopes to make smiling lips

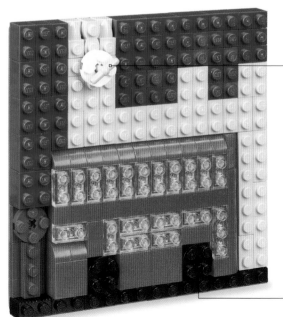

Big Ben's hands are a T-bar

Clock tower built with tooth plates

Layer plates to add detail, like the transparent windows on this red bus

CITYSCAPE

Lots of unusual bricks are used in this London cityscape. The clock tower, tree, and red bus are all built using a variety of bricks. How inventive can you be?

Wheels are round plates

FRONT VIEW

CLASSIC BOARD GAMES

Classic board games can provide hours of fun. LEGO board games are no different—and they are ideal for long journeys because the pieces stay in place! All you need is a simple base and some game pieces. Don't know the rules? Ask your family or look online. You can even adapt the game to suit your favorite theme.

FINALLY, IT'S MY CHANCE TO CAPTURE THE KING!

Each side has eight pawns, two knights, two rooks, two bishops, one king, and one queen

TOP VIEW

CHESS

A 16x16 base is a good size for lots of board games, including chess. If you don't have a baseplate, you can build one with overlapping plates to create a square. Then add eight rows of eight 2x2 plates in alternate colors to create a chessboard.

A standard chessboard has black and white squares, but you can use any colors you want!

CHECKMATE!
The chess pieces—pawns, knights, rooks, bishops, queens, and kings—should be easy to distinguish. Will your queen have a big crown? Maybe your knight will have shining armor? Make sure the pieces are sturdy because they will be moved around a lot.

1x1 plate with vertical clip

Tooth plate for a horse's nose

| Pawn | Bishop | Knight | King | Queen | Rook | | Pawn | Bishop | Knight | King | Queen | Rook |

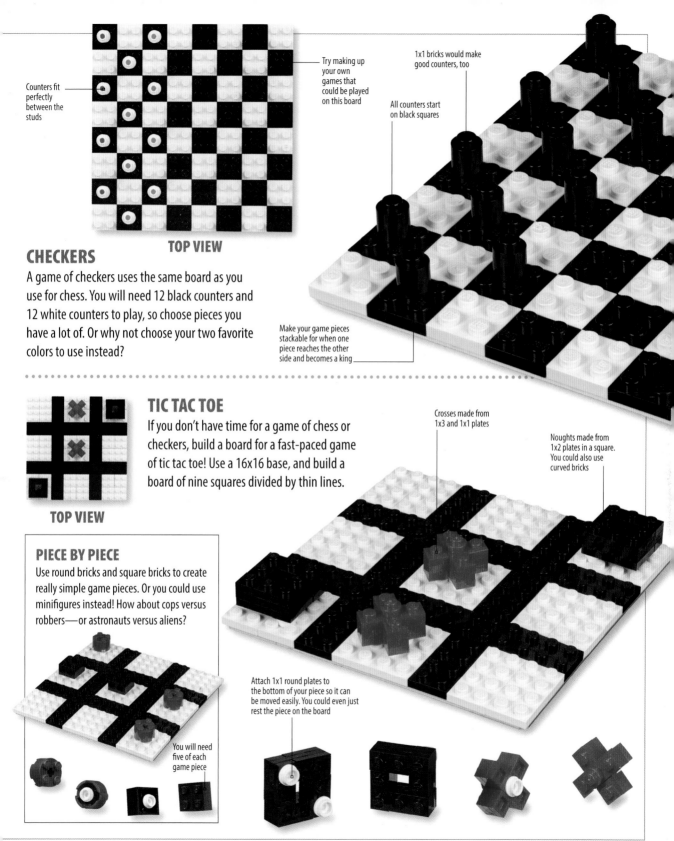

Counters fit perfectly between the studs

Try making up your own games that could be played on this board

1x1 bricks would make good counters, too

All counters start on black squares

TOP VIEW

CHECKERS

A game of checkers uses the same board as you use for chess. You will need 12 black counters and 12 white counters to play, so choose pieces you have a lot of. Or why not choose your two favorite colors to use instead?

Make your game pieces stackable for when one piece reaches the other side and becomes a king

TIC TAC TOE

If you don't have time for a game of chess or checkers, build a board for a fast-paced game of tic tac toe! Use a 16x16 base, and build a board of nine squares divided by thin lines.

Crosses made from 1x3 and 1x1 plates

Noughts made from 1x2 plates in a square. You could also use curved bricks

TOP VIEW

PIECE BY PIECE

Use round bricks and square bricks to create really simple game pieces. Or you could use minifigures instead! How about cops versus robbers—or astronauts versus aliens?

Attach 1x1 round plates to the bottom of your piece so it can be moved easily. You could even just rest the piece on the board

You will need five of each game piece

MORE BOARD GAMES

Now that you can build board games out of bricks, you and your friends will never be bored again! You can make all your favorite games, and even make up your own. Before you start building, try to organize the pieces you need. Think about how many people are going to play and what colors you want to use. You could even use your favorite minifigures as pieces.

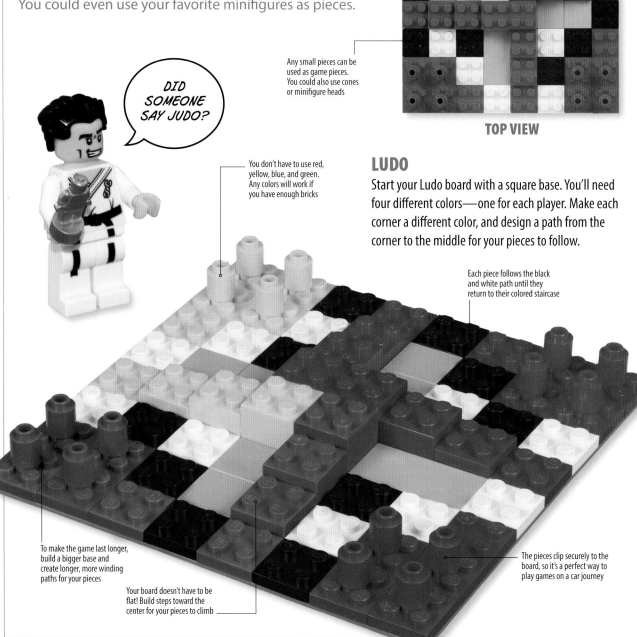

Any small pieces can be used as game pieces. You could also use cones or minifigure heads

TOP VIEW

DID SOMEONE SAY JUDO?

You don't have to use red, yellow, blue, and green. Any colors will work if you have enough bricks

LUDO

Start your Ludo board with a square base. You'll need four different colors—one for each player. Make each corner a different color, and design a path from the corner to the middle for your pieces to follow.

Each piece follows the black and white path until they return to their colored staircase

To make the game last longer, build a bigger base and create longer, more winding paths for your pieces

Your board doesn't have to be flat! Build steps toward the center for your pieces to climb

The pieces clip securely to the board, so it's a perfect way to play games on a car journey

SUMMIT

Try making up your own game. This one's called Summit because the aim of the game is to reach the top of the mountain. Build your board like a spiraling pyramid, with a path that gets a step higher each time it goes round a corner.

The winner is the first to reach the square at the top

TOP VIEW

COLOR CRAZY

Choose one or two colors to use as the default board. This model uses red and white. Every so often, substitute a different color for a square on the board to add rewards and pitfalls to the game.

You could place a flag or a treasure piece at the summit

You don't have to stick to a mountain shape. How about a castle shape where the first to reach the top is crowned king or queen?

Make up your own rules. For example, if you land on a black square you miss a go and if you land on a blue square, you move forward three spaces

BUILDING REALITY

You may have built lots of fantasy models to play with, from flying saucers to pirate ships. But now it's time to face reality! Recreating everyday household items is a different challenge, since you can pick up the real thing and take a good look before planning the best way to make it. Create life-sized models or minifigure-scale objects—it's up to you!

BUILDING BRIEF
Objective: Recreate household objects
Use: Decorative, storage
Features: Distinctive shapes, life-size
Extras: Ironing board, toaster

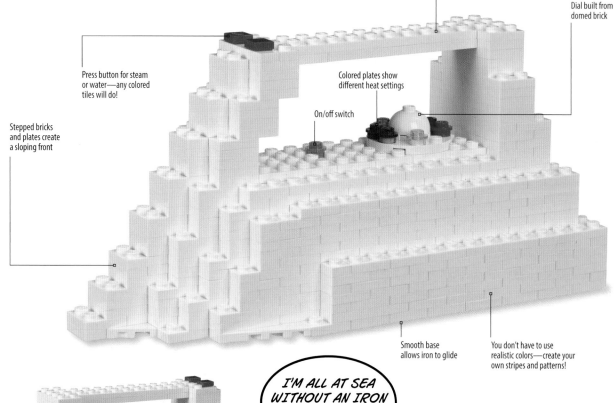

If you want to play with your iron, add more bricks or plates to the handle to make it more stable

Dial built from domed brick

Press button for steam or water—any colored tiles will do!

Colored plates show different heat settings

On/off switch

Stepped bricks and plates create a sloping front

Smooth base allows iron to glide

You don't have to use realistic colors—create your own stripes and patterns!

I'M ALL AT SEA WITHOUT AN IRON TO PRESS MY CLOTHES!

IRON

Copying the curved and sloping shape of an iron with LEGO pieces is a challenge, but it can be done! Add dials, lights, and buttons to bring your model to life—without the fear of burning your clothes! Just make sure any real iron is turned off and unplugged before you touch it!

REAR SIDE VIEW

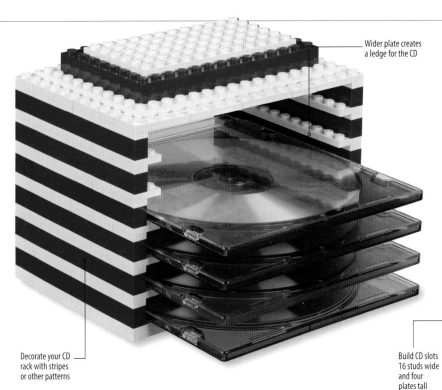

Wider plate creates a ledge for the CD

CD RACK

Sometimes LEGO builds are so realistic, they can function like the real thing! This CD rack is big and sturdy enough to hold your CD collection. Build two walls on opposite sides of a base, adding wider plates at regular intervals for your CDs to rest on.

Decorate your CD rack with stripes or other patterns

Build CD slots 16 studs wide and four plates tall

REAR SIDE VIEW

SALT AND PEPPER

These shakers can be the beginning of your LEGO dining experience. Try and recreate what might be on a dining table, from crockery to silverware, or even a candelabra!

Holes in the bricks mean that these models don't hold real-life salt and pepper!

Corner bricks surround a central column of two stacks of 1x1 bricks

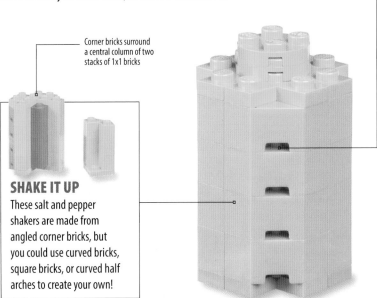

SHAKE IT UP

These salt and pepper shakers are made from angled corner bricks, but you could use curved bricks, square bricks, or curved half arches to create your own!

YOUR OWN DESIGNS

Now it's time to create some beautiful household objects using your own imagination! Instead of copying something directly, build a LEGO masterpiece of your own design. Use your favorite colors to build a decorative sculpture, or think up original designs for a set of coasters that you can use—for cold drinks only!

Mixing round and rectangular bricks helps create a curve

BUILDING BRIEF

Objective: Create objects of your own design

Use: Decorative, storage

Features: Life-size, beautiful, functional, unusual shapes, fun patterns

Extras: Paper tray, placemats, jewelry

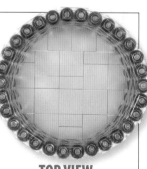

This sculpture is delicate. Can you think of a way to make it more stable?

Secure the round plates and cones with 1x2 bricks and plates

COLORFUL SCULPTURE

Stack rows of round plates, rectangular plates, cones, and bricks to make your sculpture as tall or short as you like. Choose your own colors and patterns to match the color of the room you will display the sculpture in. You could even try building different shaped sculptures.

BACK TO BASICS

Build a circular base using plates covered with tiles. At four points around the edge, position 1x2 plates and jumper plates, to which you can attach the circular sides.

TOP VIEW